MW01293208

Thank You!

TO: _____
FROM: _____

better notes

© Better Notes · Kochhannstr. 30 · 10249 Berlin · info@betternotes.de · www.betternotes.de
Author and cover design: ilyamalyanov.com

Made in United States
North Haven, CT
31 May 2022

19674535R00067